Stock Market Investing: A Beginners Guide to Investing in Stocks Successfully

Michael Joshua

DEDICATION

I would like to dedicate this book to all the newbie stock market investors. May this book provide you with a high-level overview of what you should look into before making investments in the stock market, as it should be looked at as a long-term plan and not a get rich quick scheme.

CONTENTS

ACKNOWLEDGMENTS

There is a lot of money to be made and lost in the market. Being in the finance industry myself, I get asked about stocks all the time. I figured I would put some useful information into a guide that I can provide to newbies asking the questions. I hope you find this guide useful and you will provide positive feedback and ratings on Amazon for other readers as well.

I would like to acknowledge the fact that I am not telling you what to invest in, nor telling you what not to invest in within the pages of this book. The intent of this book is to be a short read guide to providing you with a high-level overview of what information you should research on your own before dumping a bunch of money into the ever changing stock market. It is meant to be an overview of stock market investing, not an in depth look at actual stocks. Within its pages, I give you names of online brokers and resources, but you should look into further to get the confidence you need to successfully invest in the stock market.

CHAPTER 1: GETTING STARTED

We all might know about the basic concepts of investing; sometime during our lives, we might even have probably done it. For example, we invested our time in our studies to get the best grades; we invested in our relationships to nurture them, and so on; there are many more examples.

We have been doing this all our lives and so, it's not a new thing for us. But what is new for some of us is the subject of stock market investing.

Majority of the people don't know about Stock Market Investing. Let's just start with the famous Wall Street saying;

"Buy Low, sell high"

That is exactly what stock market investing is all about. You buy a stock at $10 and wait for its price to increase. As soon as you see that the price has risen far enough, for example $50, you'll sell it, making a clean $40 profit. But that was just one share.

Imagine what your profit would have been, had you sold 1000 stocks. The profit would have been a hefty amount. This thrill is what attracts many investors to stock market investing but the case is not always the same.

In some cases, the stock price might fall way below the minimum rate and people have been known to suffer losses of billions of dollars.

But let's not go there right now. Since you have already made up your mind about investing in the market, you'll need some advice on where to start.

The beginning might seem quite simple but if you want good returns on your investments, you'll need to pay attention to every minor detail. After all, it's your money and you wouldn't want to throw it away.

So just start with the first point and you'll understand all that you need to know about the basics.

✓ Determine If You Have the Resources to Invest In the Market

This might sound a bit too obvious, since you have already decided to trade in shares. But there's good reason to mention this point. Even though it might seem like you have enough to buy share, it's good to evaluate the assets again.

Have you added the broker's fee in the overall expenses? Are additional expenses added too? You might be missing something and it's still not too late to identify these hidden costs.

✓ Set the Goals That You Wish to Accomplish With the Returns

If you are thinking of investing in the stock market, it might be because you have some needs that have to be fulfilled. Make a list of the things that you wish to acquire in your life.

This bucket list will then help you set goals in life. But how does that help you in getting started with the investing? Well, it does actually.

Setting your goals and objectives will help you determine what you want from life and only by investing in the right industries will you be able to achieve that.

You might save the money for your kid's college, for a new house or maybe for that world tour you've been meaning to go on all your life.

Whatever the objective is, once you are clear about it, you'll know how far you will have to travel from your current position to accomplish it.

✓ **Are You Able to Bear the Risk Involved?**

Always keep the risk in close perspective. If you can gain $100 on the stock market, there are chances that you can also lose more than that. So before you start trading stocks, it's advisable that you determine what your risk tolerance is.

And if any stock's profile does not conform to that level, it's better that you don't invest in that particular stock. Taking undue risk might prove to be more harmful than you have imagined.

Since you are a newbie, it's better to keep a low profile and invest in stocks that promise good returns, with low risks.

✓ **Research and Increase Your Knowledge about the Market that you would like to Invest in**

You're in for a new challenge and for that, you need to be geared up and ready to take on the market. So before you begin investing in the stocks, you need to gather as much knowledge about the market as you can.

Read about the stocks that you are interested in and what rules and policies govern the markets you would like to operate in. There are many chances that the economy at large, might be in trouble and thus, investing in stocks at that time may be more harmful than useful.

Apart from reading, listen to what the experts are saying about the market. Market analysts predict about the market and based on their knowledge and experience, these predictions come true most of the time.

So listen to their insights and you will be able to understand what goes on in the market and how you can succeed at investing in stocks.

✓ **Classic Investment Books**

Don't know where to start? Well, take guidelines from some of the classic investment books, mentioned below.

- **How to make money in stocks**, by William O'Neil
- **One up on Wall St**, by Peter Lynch
- **Buffet: The Making of an American Capitalist**, by Roger Lowenstein
- **The Theory of Investment Value,** by John Burr Williams
- **Reminiscences of a stock operator,** by Edwin Lefevre
- **Market Wizards,** by Jack Schwager
- **A Random Walk Down Wall Street,** by Burton G. Malkeil

- **The Intelligent Investor and Security Analysis** by Benjamin Graham
- **The Little Book of Common Sense Investing,** by Jack Bogle
- **Liar's Poker,** by Michael Lewis
- **The Interpretation of Financial Statements** by Benjamin Graham and Spencer B. Meredith.
- **The Alchemy of Finance,** by George Soros
- **Common Stocks and Uncommon Profits,** by Philip A. Fisher

✓ **Focus and Think of Some Contingency Plans in Case Something Goes Wrong**

There's no guarantee as to what might happen in the stock market. Even if you invest wisely, there are chances that some things might go wrong and you end up with nothing to show for all the efforts.

This is not to scare you away from investing but this will just help you think of a contingency plan in case things don't go as you planned.

The best way to do that would be to not invest all your money in the same stocks. Some contingency plans will come up in the later topics but you do get the idea. Just know a way out, in case something doesn't turn out to be good.

CHAPTER 2: FINDING A BROKER

The next step would be to understand what brokers are and what services they can provide you with. Well, it's quite simple actually. If you want to trade stocks, then a stock broker will become one of the most important people in your life.

This professional will buy or sell stocks and other securities, through the stock exchange or over the counter.

✓ **Types of Brokers**

They generally fall into three categories;

- **Advisory or Full service brokers:** As the name implies, these agents will advise and discuss investment ideas with you, although you do get to make the final decision. For clients with large portfolios, advisory brokers also offer discretionary services, where they manage the client's money for them.

  Many people do avail these services but it is advised that the broker must be trust worthy and legitimate before you let them handle all your money.

  In return of these exclusive services, advisory brokers charge more but many investors don't mind as long as they get the insight and the additional support.

- **Execution-only or discount brokers:** These brokers will just trade the shares whenever and with whatever share you want them to, without providing any extra support. All they do is carry out your trading instructions, either on phone or online.

✓ **What you must look for when finding a broker**

There are many details to pay attention to once have decided to invest in the stock market. Since you are not a professional trader, you'll need to gather as much information as you can before you even start to trade.

Here are a few pointers that you must keep in mind before you hire a broker. Also review the issues that you might have to face after hiring your broker.

- **They must be licensed as a broker**

You wouldn't want just anyone to be in charge of your life's savings. Of course, no one would want that. That's why it's vital that you do a lot of research when choosing your broker. Get in touch with the people who already trade in stocks. They will know more about brokers and brokerage firms than you do and will be able to give you valuable advice.

Your job would then be to ensure that the broker or the brokerage firm has been licensed by the governing authorities. Since there are many cases of fraud in stock market dealings, you should work with someone who is legitimate and has the expertise.

- ## Minimum balance for an Account

Many brokers have set minimum balances for the accounts of investors. If you want to start a brokerage account, you might need to deposit of a certain specified amount in the account. Only then will you be able to trade stocks.

Usually, the minimum amount is $500 - $1000 but this amount is for online brokerages. If you are dealing with a broker, make sure that your brokerage account fulfills the minimum requirements.

- ## Withdrawal charges of the Broker

This might sound quite surprising, but it turns out to be true sometimes. Even though the account is yours, all the money invested is yours, and even the broker has been hired by you; some of the brokers charge fees to make a withdrawal.

In other cases, they might not let you withdraw any money if the account's balance gets below the minimum set point.

There's nothing much you can do about it once you have gotten into a contract with the broker. So before you sign up, it's important to read the fine print and understand all the policies regarding withdrawing money from an account.

- ## The biggest Fish in the sea might not be worth your while

Each broker has their own specialty and that's where you need to be careful when selecting a broker. Some brokers are more suitable for professional traders while others are geared up to help the beginners.

Here, you'll need to help yourself and select the broker that can assist you the best. Selecting a famous broker might not give you the leverage that having an intermediate level broker might. They'll have more time to help you out and they will ensure that your money grows rapidly.

- **Understand the Fee Structures**

Your broker's fee structure might look quite innocent but there's no telling if there are any hidden fees somewhere in the agreement or not. Brokers display easy-to-pay fee structures to attract customers.

If your broker proposes an unusual fee structure, make sure that there's nothing hidden below the surface. It's better to make sure of everything before you get hit by a swarm of additional hidden charges.

So read all the account agreements and contracts before you establish a professional relationship with your broker.

✓ **Online Brokerages**

These online firms are providing traders with all the services of a broker but that is all done online. You get to save time, get valuable information right from your workplace and there is no need to visit your broker every time you need help.

With online brokerages, all these services are available to you from wherever you want and whenever you need them. Whatever your investment style, you're sure to find a brokerage that will cater to your needs.

But a word of caution; people usually just decide on an online broker and rely on the advertisements to speak for the broker's reliability. But that is not always the case.

Anybody can pay for advertisements to run 24/7, it's not too hard.

But not all online brokers are efficient enough to deal with your money the way you would prefer.

So before you decide on any broker, it's better that you do some kind of research about them, making sure that your objectives are aligned with those of the broker.

If you are having trouble deciding who your broker should be, you can just visit http://www.timothysykes.com/preferred-broker/ and find out who your preferred broker should be. All you would have to do is fill a form and the site's team will tell you what online broker you should hire.

Listed below are the names of 5 top online brokers, some of which excel in giving excellent customer service while others possess strong trading tools. Whatever their strong points are, it's your decision, so choose wisely.

You wouldn't want to get stuck with a broker that invests your money unwisely.

- **ETRADE:** This easy to use trading platform uses powerful tools that make it stand out in the crowd of online brokers. Clients get a dashboard that they can customize according to their specification and this is the feature that won ETRADE "Best Client Dashboard" award.

  The site's mobile App was rated "#1 Smartphone App" in the StockBrokers.com 2015 Broker Review. So if you are in need of expert broker services, ETRADE should be your first choice.

- **Fidelity:** Having been awarded "Best in Class" in six categories, Fidelity Investments received 4.5 out of 5 stars in 2015 review of stockbroker.com. They are located at 180 retail locations and have been awarded the "Best iPad App" award in 2013.

  With such honors, it's easy to say that Fidelity Investments will take care of all your financial requirements

- **TD Ameritrade:** Featuring two platforms; Thinkorswim, which was ranked "#1 Desktop Platform" in 2014' and Trade Architect, TD Ameritrade offers its clients a host of specialized services. These platforms are loaded with features.

  Adding to the benefits is the TD Ameritrade's education, investment guidance, robust research and many more tools that facilitate clients to make the best investments. So when you are dealing through TD Ameritrade, you'll have the peace of mind of having hired the best online brokers there are.

- **Merrill Edge:** In 2015, Merrill Edge was awarded #1 for Banking Services. Clients are offered a vast array of services that makes it quite convenient for them to trade. They are directly linked to the Bank of America and are considered the Best in Class for research, Customer service, Investor Education and Banking.

- **OptionsHouse:** Being ranked #1 for Options Trading in the StockBrokers.com 2015 Broker Review, should be enough to assure you that you'll be dealing with one of the best brokers in the market.

  Their easy to use web based platform, tradeMONSTER is known to get clients simple and discounted trading services. Opting for OptionsHouse will ensure that you get the specialized services you want.

- **Charles Schwab:** Rated#1 for retirement servicers, Charles Schwab is a great service brokerage that provides specialized services to their clients such as, extensive research access, efficient customer service and banking services. It's a sure bet that Charles Schwab will not disappoint you at all.

- **Scottrade:** What could be the best service? One that provides its customers with the Best Overall Client Experience 2015. And how was that possible? The specialized services and strong trading tools have enabled the site's clients to trade in stocks easily and in the best way they can.

  They have over 500 local branch offices for personal service that is the largest network operated by an online broker service. This one of a kind service makes Scottrade outshine other online brokers.

  So be assured that availing this service will help you get rid of any ambiguities about stock market investing.

- **TradeStation:** Though it is an advanced trading platform, it's advised that beginners should also just a look at all the benefits of using TradeStation. They have been awarded "Best Platform Technology" in 2013 and 2014 and is considered "Best in Class" for Platform & Tools, Active trading, Options trading.

- **TradeKing:** Currently scoring a customer service rating of 4.0, TradeKing is on the way to become of the top notch online brokers. They offer investors competitive trade commissions, extensive research for stocks, mutual funds and many more high quality services.

  All you would have to do is just sign up with the corporation and they will take care that none of your investments go to waste. Not only that, their Trade Network enables investors to share their ideas, investment guidelines and stories, market research and analysis. This helps all the investors cumulatively and doesn't even cost you more!

- **Capital One Investing:** A perfect fit for casual investors, they are known for their convenient automatic investment plans. They have discounted automatic trade commissions, which are less expensive than other online brokers. And because of their impressive Online Banking Services, they were awarded #1 in 2014.

Well, those were some of the fast growing online brokers that have earned the respect of their clients by offering specialized platforms, easy to use mobile apps or by providing exceptional customer service and support. So decide on one of those brokers or better yet, do some research of your own and start investing in the stocks like a pro.

CHAPTER 3: COMPARE ONLINE BROKERS

As we have previously discussed, you should not go with the first broker you hear of. But why? That's simple enough. You are investing your hard earned money in the stocks.

Some people even invest all of their lives' saving to gain profit at the stock market. Then how can you choose someone that is not capable of dealing with the responsibility? Surely you'll want a broker who knows what the stakes are and who will work hard to not get any losses in your account.

My decision will vary from yours and that's natural. You might not find a broker compatible while I might find them to be the best broker I can get. All of this depends on our specific investing needs.

You might be more interested in investing in the IT industry while I might have my eyes on Pharmaceutical. Both of us hiring the same broker might not be the right choice because the industry dynamics are totally different.

What might be best for the Pharmaceutical Industry might negatively affect the IT industry. Simply put, the needs of both the industries are different and so it'll be more profitable for us to look for a broker that specializes in the certain market.

Specialized broker? You might wonder what that is. Brokers deal with stocks of all the industries, at the same time. But with the changing economic conditions and the diversity in the industry dynamics, it's better to get a broker that might have greater knowledge of the specific industry you want to operate in. But if you are not particular about the industry that you'd like to invest in, just go for the broker that you deem compatible enough.

Even then, a broker must satisfy some factors to qualify as an efficient broker. What are those? Just read on to know what you must expect from a broker and what criteria they must satisfy.

✓ Customer Service:

Dealing with virtual brokers might not satisfy your investment needs the way an actual, human broker would. But you don't need to worry about that. All the top notch online brokers have well trained customer service professionals that are willing to help you with any issue that you have.

So the first thing that you must look for when comparing online brokers is online assistance at all hours. If you have to choose between a broker that offers assistance and another one that can only be reached through mail and even then takes several days to respond, the choice should be quite obvious.

It's your money at stake here. You wouldn't want an unprofessional individual to manage your lives' savings. Some of the above mentioned online brokers have award winning customer services so you should definitely check them out.

✓ International Trading:

You might enthusiastically search for brokers and might come up with half a dozen on a list within minutes. This effort would greatly encourage you and you might seven pat yourself on the back at how efficiently your search engine came up with the answers. But did you stop to consider in what nation the brokers operate in. It might have not come to you at that time but go back and consider this.

Now you'll find that maybe half of the brokers on the list were from a different country. Had you not paid attention to this on time, you might have found yourself investing in the stocks of Uganda. The key point is, when comparing brokers, make sure that they offer services in your country.

✓ **Market Research**

This might be your first time investing in the stock market and you'll need all the help that you can get. So you're on the lookout for an online broker that possesses extensive market knowledge and one who provides you with a variety of market research tools.

Not all them are going to be free, of course, but they will nevertheless be helpful as you trade stocks. The simple fact being, the more you pay per trade, the more access you can obtain to the market research data of the online broker.

From the above mentioned online brokers, **TD Ameritrade** and **Etrade** provide their customers with extensive market research, helping them with stock market investing.

✓ **Account Security**

In the past two years, many big corporations have been a victim of cybercrime and that has resulted in loss for thousands of people. To ensure the safety of each and every transaction of their customers, online brokers invest heavily into account security. And that surely is the right thing to do. After all, it's your money that would be at stake if there was any threat of cybercrime.

So do look for an online broker that is well known to have a secured account and who is ready to invest in it. Always choose an established broker for your portfolio so any mishaps can be avoided.

✓ **Investment Options**

An ideal online broker must give you the freedom to trade in whatever security you want, whether it is trading stocks, mutual Funds, ETFs or options. Whatever you decide to invest in, the broker should be ready and must have the resources to help you invest.

Although most of the online brokers give you this chance but there are some who have a limited investment portfolio. OptionsXpress and MB Trading offer invest options in all the mentioned securities and additionally, even in forex and futures trading.

✓ **Trade Commissions**

Being a newbie, you might find yourself being charged quite hefty amounts. So be on the lookout for online brokers who charge way over the original price. Find out what it costs to buy stocks and whether that is the same amount being charged by your online broker.

The fees charged by the broker varies with each company so find out whether each transaction is being charged based on the type of order or the size of order.

✓ **Retirement Accounts**

Many brokers are adamant about setting up retirement accounts for their customers. These accounts usually have convenient features that facilitate users, such as one click access between different accounts.

Though these accounts might seem a good idea at the time, watch out for brokers who might be charging overheads and yearly fees that amount to a hefty balance at the end of the year.

You'll want to reap all the benefits of hiring a broker. So if that comes with a retirement account, who would complain?

✓ Banking

Online brokers are not just your ticket to the top of stock market as they have now started offering their clients banking and other financial services too. Some well-established brokers provide their clients with checking accounts, and there are even some brokers who have been handing out credit cards.

So if you can get specialized brokerage services along with banking services, why not go for that option? If you would like to save money, then it's advised that you look for brokers who offer all these services.

✓ Trading Tools

In the fast paced world of today, it's crucial that you take right decisions at the right time. So when you select your broker, make sure that they make use of the latest tools for trading. A top broker will provide you access to a large variety of trade tools so you can get the best out of each and every transaction.

Having strong trading tools will make trading a successful venture and active investors will be able to gain benefits off real time streamers to last sales ticker, mobile trading and live news feed. So if your broker has the essential tools that can add value to your investment, then they are the right broker for you.

✓   **Speed & Execution**

Stock market is all about timing; you can suffer a loss of millions if you let that moment pass by, but you can also gain billions if you managed to take the right decision on time. For active traders, speed and active execution is crucial.

Some brokers might not give such significance to time and you might lose a lot of money just because of that. There are noticeable differences in each broker's speed and execution of a transaction. So if you don't want to end up suffering a loss that will put all your gains in perspective, select a broker who understands the value of time and speed.

CHAPTER 4: MAKING YOUR INVESTMENTS

Now that you are finally done with all the research; it's time to start making use of that money. If you have opted for an automatic investment system, then you need not worry about the upcoming pointers.

But if you have decided to go into the battle field alone, then I advise you to hang on to every word that is included hereafter.

✓ **Allocate your assets**

Starting at the first step; you are not making any investments right now. All you have to do at this point is allocate your resources. Just think about how much money you are going to invest in the stock market.

Here, you'll need to take caution. After all, it's the stock market; you never know what the next day might bring your way. If you are thinking of making an initial investment more than what you can afford to lose, keep in mind that there is equal risk on both sides.

In my opinion, it'll be better if you just start slow, making small investments at first until you get used to the idea.

So decided carefully and allocate your resources to the stocks where you would like to invest. Divide the desired resources into parts and decide what securities you would want to invest in.

Whether you'll be going for stocks or bonds, or aggressive alternatives and how much you will invest in cash equivalents such as, certificates of deposit, Treasury bills, etc.

✓ Evaluate the Company

Get to know the company before you invest; do some research and get the numbers of their latest ventures. When you look at the company's financial statements, i.e. the balance sheet and income statement, you need to pay attention to some key points.

These figures will help you choose the best company to invest in.

- **Earnings**
  This number should be at least 10 percent higher than the year before.

- **Price to Sales Ratio (PSR)**
  This number should be as close to 1 as possible.

- **Debt**
  The overall debt of the company should be lower than the year before and if not lower, it must at least be at the same level. Also, check that the debts must be less than the total assets of the company.

- **Equity**
  Total equities of the company must have increased in number

as compared to the year before.

- **Return on equity (ROE)**
  This number should constantly be increasing at least 10 percent each year.

- **Sales**
  Sales should have increased this year as compared to last year. The margin doesn't really matter but if a company has increased more than 10 percent of sales, they might be eligible to invest in.

✓ **Information Sources to help you evaluate a company**

There are a number of things that can help you assess the financial position and stability of a company. Some might be helpful in one situation but might be quite worthless in other situations. Nevertheless, here is a list of the most common sources.

- **Business Journals and Magazines**
  These journals and magazines might be your best source of portraying a company's financial health. They collect business and industry news, which eventually helps investors in assessing the companies they might be interested in.

- **Annual Reports**
  Annual reports show the financial statements of the company and project its financial standing. You can learn a lot by looking at a company's annual reports. Though these might help you evaluate the company, many people might not know how to use all that data.

- **Industry Sources**
  You might get whatever information you need from industry experts and sources but there's no saying if the information is true or not.

Even if you have a really reliable source, there could be chances that they might not be well informed about the company's true financial state. So it might not be wise to trust these sources all the time.

- **Brokerages**

It is a perception that brokers know the true state of any company and it is right on many accounts. So if you need information that is one place from where you may get the information you need.

✓ **Select the Company**

Now it's time to choose which type of stocks you are going to invest in. In order to keep a diverse portfolio, you'll have to choose from growth stocks or dividend stocks. These stock investment strategies are going to determine your earning pattern. So let's take a look at what these two options offer.

- **Growth stocks**

    This follows the basic principle of stock market investing; buying a stock when it is low and selling it when it's worth a lot. These stocks might earn you a lot; always choose a company that has room to expand and grow.

    But growth stocks can be quite volatile. Every now and then, you might hear of people losing all their money in the stock market. It only happens when they over-invest in a high risk company.

    So if you are planning on investing in growth stocks, you'll need to be quite careful and must have an insight on how well the company is doing at the moment. You should always buy stocks that have had the chance to prove themselves and show great potential.

If growth stocks seem too risky to you and are not your cup of tea, then it is better to invest in dividend stocks.

- **Dividend Stocks**

  Dividend stocks are a better and safer way to earn money in the stock market. The idea here is to invest in companies that pay dividend and thus, are more stable than growth stocks.

  These companies have mostly reached their maturity stage and their growth is slow. But the plus point is that these stocks will earn you dividend every month.

  These stocks are the ideal choice for young investors who are looking for a source of income in the long run or for people who are about to retire. This lower risk investment opportunity is best to generate more money in the long haul.

The best investment would be a mixture of both Growth stocks and Dividend Stocks because of course, investing in a single stock leads directly to financial ruin. So keep a clear head when investing.

✓ **Value the Stocks**

Now you need to know the true value of the decided company's stock. This might get a bit technical so you might want to get the help of someone who has done this before.

Valuation of stocks can be done using any one of the techniques described below.

- **Dividend Discount Model**

  The first method is called the **Dividend Discount Model** and it means that the value of the stock is the present value of all its future dividends. Just calculate the difference between the discount rate of a share and the dividend growth rate. Divide the Dividend per share with this value and you'll know the actual value of the stock.

It's better explained with an example. If a company pays a dividend of $2 on every share and is expected to increase with a growth rate of 10% each year and the discount rate is 12%; then the stock is worth $100 per share.

- **Discounted Cash Flow Model**
  The **Discounted Cash Flow Model** states that the value of a stock is the present value of all its future cash flows.

- **Comparable Methods:**
  The easiest way is to use the **Comparable Methods** where you evaluate a stock based on its price compared to sales (P/S), book value (P/B), earnings (P/E) or cash flow (P/CF).

  A benchmark is provided and you just have to compare the given values with the stock's historic average ratios. Once done, you'll know at what price the stock should sell.

✓ **Purchase the stocks**

After you have successfully evaluated the value of the stocks you would like to invest in, it's time to put it to use. Now it's time to finally put all that research into practice.

Yes, you can now purchase the stock that best suits your investment purpose. If you are dealing through an online brokerage, just inform them where you'll like to invest and it'll be done in no time at all.

Some companies have **Direct Stock Purchase Plans (DSPPs)**; this plan allows you to purchase their stocks without even dealing with a broker. Do some research and you'll get the names of all the companies that offer such programs.

✓ Ensure diversity in your investments

Do keep in mind that you need to keep the costs as low as possible to ensure that the returns are higher. And make sure that you have a vast variety of stocks.

You can get stocks from different sectors and industries; this will make sure that all your earnings won't go down if one industry experiences a sudden decrease. Invest in stocks from different companies from other countries just to ensure that all your money doesn't get stuck in one place.

Remember that a diverse portfolio is the key to succeeding in the stock market. Also, keep a healthy number of growth and dividend stocks; the latter to earn you a stable income in the long term.

✓ Don't go for short term investments, invest for long term

You might feel the urge to sell the stocks if the market goes down, especially if it has been experiencing this for quite some time. But selling might not be the right option at this time. The stock market is always profitable in the long run, so even if the stocks see a tremendous increase, it's better not to cash on the benefits.

However, you can do this if you really need the money and the market is steadily growing. Another reason to sell the stock could be if the company has lost its ability to outperform anymore. But if you really want to benefit from the stock market, keep your eyes on the long term benefits.

✓ Make an investment pattern to invest regularly

It simply wouldn't be profitable for you if you invest in some stocks and just forget about them. Make an investment pattern and decide when to invest each month. If you are seriously considering earning from the stock market; then you will need to set aside some money from each paycheck to go into investing.

If you see a decrease in the stock market, then invest more in the stocks. This might seem unwise but believe me; this is the best time to buy stocks. But you'll ask why? There's a simple enough reason for that.

Stock market has the tendency to fall quickly but it also rises with the same speed. It always gets back on track though it might take some time. So if your stocks are falling rapidly, you might want to hold onto them for a little while longer and just see where that will take you.

It would be wise if you keep track of the company's actions and the latest happenings. If you still feel that the company might not perform well, then trust your intuition and sell the stocks.

✓ Make an exit strategy

You must keep a clear eye on the stocks. Here, we must establish an extremely important point; your ultimate should always be long term investments but that is not the only type of stock you must deal in.

You need to have a number of stocks that you trade regularly but not too frequently. These stocks will be your key to some quick and easy profits. But how will that work? Quite easily actually!

If a stock's price falls, you might consider buying some more stocks but only if the fundamentals of the stock remain strong. The price will eventually rise and you will make a clean cut profit.

In another scenario, if the fundamentals of a company don't look so good and the price is high, get out before it collapses because of the unsound conditions. You must develop a clear and precise exit strategy but this might vary with the situation. So be alert and assess the situation as best as you can.

CHAPTER 5: MAINTAINING YOUR PORTFOLIO

Brokers usually offer you this service; they keep track of all your investments and buy stocks from diverse companies and countries, just so that you can have a widespread portfolio.

Maintaining a portfolio will help you earn money in the long term. Leaving your stock portfolio for your broker to decide is an option, but if you would prefer to do it yourself, then there are many tools that can help you in achieving that.

✓ Set Up Benchmarks

You must have had some expectations with the stocks that you invested in and if they get fulfilled, then you will be earning worth your investment. But how will you know if the stocks do meet your expectations or not?

You'll have to set some benchmarks to measure the stock's performance. Determine how much growth each stock requires to make it worth keeping. You can use the market indexes to measure the performance; this will tell you whether the company is performing as well as the other companies, in the same sector.

As I've mentioned before, you have to look at the long term goals and not make hasty decisions. If you see that your investments are not performing as well as you expected them to, you could sell them.

But make sure whether these setbacks are going to last long or whether they are due to some new trend in the market. You'll have to dig up information about it. If your research shows that the company might be in trouble for a long time, then be wise and sell the shares before you lose all your investment.

There are no hard and fast rules as to when to sell shares. It all depends on the situation and you are the best judge of that, although you can get some really helpful tips in the coming chapters.

✓ Use Online Tools

There are some stocks that can only be bought through licensed brokers and this might cause problems for you in maintaining your portfolio. But if you have access to online tools, then you can easily overcome any of the problems.

These tools come at a range of prices and offer vast number of services; you'll just need to choose what best suits your investment needs. These tools can include graphics, which will enable you to see and measure growth or losses over a certain period of time.

✓ Design a Schedule

Managing a stock portfolio not only requires time but also takes a lot of efforts. You wouldn't want to be caught up in the middle of chaos so it's better that you manage things properly, right from the start.

You can hire someone to keep track of all your investments. It might cost you a bit but doing so will surely get things off your hands and you'll get to spend that time doing other things. Make a schedule and mark the days which you will spend in maintaining your portfolio each month.

Also, decide how long you would hold onto a stock and how soon you need to sell a certain, low performing stock.

One of my colleagues was interested in investing and I showed him the basics and he started off soon after. He was quite efficient in his investments and soon, he had set up quite an impressive portfolio.

The returns were good and he was also earning dividends on many of the stocks. All was good but soon, he started a new job that didn't leave him with much time to check on his portfolio. I fully expected him to start losing money soon but he was not about to let all his efforts go to waste.

Since he wasn't able to check on his investments for some time, he lost quite a few shares and had to sell some too. Then he hired an assistant who checked up on his investment portfolio and since he had invested in some great projects, he was able to afford it.

The point of the whole story being that your carelessness could very well make you end up where you started. He was lucky but that might not always be the case.

✓ **Keep Records of All Transactions**

You must have proof of every transaction that you have ever made. You must have hard copies of all the stocks that you hold and have held in the past. You might have all this information on your online accounts but just to be on the safe side, it is better that you keep receipts and transaction information in the form of hard copies.

Also, keep track of the cost of an online broker and keep the payment receipts. These expenses can be deducted from your income tax, but only if you managed to add them up accurately.

✓ **Re-examine Your Portfolio**

You cannot just buy stocks and leave them be. If you plan to do that, then prepare yourself to lose your money. I'm not trying to scare you off, it's just the truth. I know some stock market investors who made the same mistake.

They invested in the best companies, they were on their way to great fortunes but they let it all slip through their hands just because they weren't diligent. It all happened in a jiffy and they were not sure what really hit them. You might find it astonishing but that can easily happen to anyone.

I mentioned in the start that investing in stock market will take more than just money. You'll have to invest in a lot more efforts and that includes examining all the stocks that you currently hold.

Assess whether any changes have occurred or not, which usually happens quite frequently in the stock market. A share might be doing well one day and the very next hour, it might go down.

It'll help if you keep a keen eye on the stock market. But what changes must the stock go through in order for you to think about selling it? Well, there are a number of things which can contribute towards your decision of getting rid of a stock.

Changes to dividends, the time horizon within the companies and of course, yours too, will tell you that this is the right time to sell this particular stock. It's really necessary to assess your portfolio from time to time, more than you might deem it to be important.

A word of advice though, many people do sell the low performing stocks but fail to reinvest that money. That might do you more harm than good.

So be vigilant in these decisions, you wouldn't want to lose in the stock market, especially when you have so many opportunities to outperform.

✓ Don't trade excessively

I too, have been tempted to sell off some stocks whenever there are any price gyrations and so far, I've been successful in warding off these distracting thoughts. But why do I do that?

Unless you are sure that a stock is falling for good, resist the temptation to sell it. You are going to experience a lot of ups and downs in the stock market and if you jump at every time a share goes down 10 cents, you'll be jumping around a lot.

Remember than you are an investor and not a speculator. Don't let yourself be pulled into the vicious cycle. Besides that, every time you trade a share, it's going to cost you in broker's fee. And if you make a habit of trading excessively, then you'll be spending most of your profits paying brokers.

Not an ideal way to spend your earnings, is it?

Now there are a few things that might encourage you to sell off your shares frequently. One of the biggest reasons might be the stock tips that are circulated around. My advice would be to not trust any of the tit bits that you receive.

The simple fact is that people recommend the stocks of only those companies which pay them to do so, irrespective of how they might be performing. There's nothing shocking about this, it's quite a common practice for some companies but you'll have to be cautious. Don't trust these tips.

Many of my friends who invest in the stock market have a rigid schedule. The first thing they do when they wake up is to check on the stocks. Even their morning coffee comes after that. They pay too much attention to what the media is reporting and so even the tiniest disturbance in the stock market upsets them.

Don't let these things distract you; they are a common occurrence in the stock market and so there's no stopping that. But what you can do is not panic. Trust your intuition and focus on investing for the long term.

So don't let the daily price changes get you down and tempt you into ruining your chances of making it big in the stock market.

✓ Continue the learning process

Some of your new investors might have already started dealing with brokers and some might be on their way to successful investments on their own. If you are the latter one, then you will need all the help that you can get.

It goes without saying but if you ever need help, then consult an experienced broker or consultant. But that shouldn't stop you from gathering all the information you can about the market. The trends are changing rapidly and there's no saying how that will affect the market.

The best you can do is keep abreast with the news and any information you can get on investing. I mentioned a couple of books in the first chapter and they could be great help if you go through them. The main objective is to continue the learning process and get help from any source you can find.

But do make sure that the sources are reliable or else you might find yourself getting into trouble rather than gaining any profits from them.

Many experienced investors share their stories and these experts might be your ticket to successful investing opportunities. Read articles that will help you cope with the aspects of investing and how you can deal with the frequent ups and downs of the market.

The important thing is that you must know when to act and what actions you must take. You can reach this level of insight only if you have the right information and if you are willing to deal with the risks that are inherent in the stock market.

CHAPTER 6: TIPS ON SMART INVESTING

The previous chapters have told you about where to start and what to do, so as to get good profits in the stock market. Since there's no saying which move will get you the most profits in Stock markets, there are only some useful tips that you can follow to get some success in the Stock Market.

- ➤ Always remember that you are not just buying a stock, you are buying a company. So keep your eyes on the company and how well it's performing, and your stocks will earn you the profits you expect from them.

- ➤ Keep in mind that the only reason you're investing in a particular company is because it's performing financially well and you would like to be a part of the success. There's nothing more to it, so be clear about your objectives and what you expect from the company.

- ➤ The most profitable stocks might be of companies that have little or no competition. So try to look out for such companies; they might not be many but some companies like that are surely out there.

➤ The learning process will take time. If you want to start earning profit from the very next day, that might be impossible.

➤ Remember to ask yourself why you are investing in a particular stock, in fact, why are you even investing in the stock market. If you are able to answer that question with well-reasoned answers, then you might be ready to take the big step.

➤ Trust your intuition and let it be guided by expert advice. Any one of the two might not be good enough to get you the desired results.

➤ Emotions have no use in the investing business; all that you need is insight. So don't get fooled by biasness.

➤ Since this is your first time investing in the stock market, you should better prepare yourself for some small losses.

➤ You will need to keep a keen eye out for blue chips. Since they are good investments, you will need to be able to identify such companies before other investors get a whiff of them. If you successfully accomplish that, then you will be able to reap the benefits of being a 'bottom up' investor.

➤ Persistence is the key to success so don't give up too soon. The next shot might be your winning shot.

➢ The right information will take you a long way. So be vigilant and keep assessing your performance and gathered information.

➢ If you ever get a chance to buy high-quality stocks that are temporarily at low valuations, don't hold back. This might be your key to high level, valuable investing; in short, your ladder to climb up to stock market success.

➢ You'll be better off investing in companies that are more shareholder-oriented as there are many companies that will spend profits on establishing their businesses rather than paying dividends to the shareholders. So if you come across a sound dividend policy or stock option, you'll know that the company will be good to invest in.

➢ It has been repeated many times in the whole book but I would like to emphasize on this point again; invest for the long term. You will be able to beat the market if you hold stocks for some years.

➢ You might consider investing in companies that have a strong brand name, along with a strong employer branding. These companies make a good choice; such as Coca-Cola, Procter & Gamble etc.

You might panic when your stocks go down but that's never to be done. Sweating over it will do you no good, so always be confident in the quality of your investments rather than being nervous.

CHAPTER 7: PRECAUTIONS TO TAKE WHEN INVESTING

➢ Avoid volatile investments such as futures options, and foreign stocks if you feel that they might not fit your investment strategy. After all, you are the best judge of all your investments.

➢ Don't buy a stock that is less than $15 because market leaders do not offer their shares at such low prices.

➢ Don't overemphasize the price to earnings ratio, although you will need to keep an eye on it. Some investors stress over low P/E Ratio; be calm, it might not necessarily mean that the stocks are undervalued.

➢ Resist the temptation of buying penny stocks, or low-priced stocks of moderately reputed companies. The urge might be high but in case you do invest and the market falls, you might be looking at a loss of your whole investment. A $1 stock that falls even a little bit will eventually cause you more damage than any other stock.

➤ Don't worry about the taxes, but be a little concerned. If you are going to put taxes above your investments and worry about them, it might lead you to make misguided decisions. You should only be concerned about investing your money and multiplying it.

➤ Don't evaluate your portfolio more than a month. It may sound harsh but you wouldn't want to be caught up in the flare of the ongoing Wall Street changes. You might want to let go of some of your best investments, if you see them losing money but since your focus should be on the long term investment, be cautious.

CHAPTER 8: CONCLUSION

I have tried to convey all that I know about Stock Market Investing and all the information I was able to gather from extensive book reading, researching and my practical experience. I hope that whoever reads this book gets the most out of it and one day, might make it big in the stock market.

This book is something that has been on my mind since a long time and now that I have finally managed to accomplish my goal, I realize how much of a help it can be to all the newbies out there. I, too was once just like you and wouldn't have betted a dime that someday I would make it big in the frightening world of the Stock Market.

Too many of you, the Stock Market might seem like a frightening entity but that is only because you have yet to encounter the opportunities that it presents. All you need to do is believe in yourself and trust your intuitions.

There might be some times when you might feel like giving it all up but remember that you have to be persistent and that meager losses are just a small price to pay for the ultimate success that awaits you.

Some people might discourage you from investing in the Stock Market and might make you question your decision, but be persistent and go ahead once you have made it. If you have a clear investment strategy and you are willing to make some efforts; then fear not. When you have everything planned out, just go for it.

The most important thing is to take it easy. Getting excited and being irresponsible with your investments might make you lose everything that you managed to create with so much hard work.

So start investing but make sure that your taxes are in order. You don't need to obsess over taxes but do consider starting a Roth IRA or 401k, as both of these can help save a great deal in taxes.

Take it slow at first; after all, Warren Buffet started with investing in just three shares and now, look at where he is! Best of Luck!

ABOUT THE AUTHOR

Michael Joshua got his undergraduate degree in Finance and works full time at a large bank as a Financial Analyst. He has great knowledge in Business & Money, along with politics and technology.

Goodreads:
https://www.goodreads.com/user/show/46377085-michael-joshua

Twitter:
https://twitter.com/mjoshua_author